UNDERSTANDING BIBLE TOPICS

Understanding Bible topics

John Eddison

SCRIPTURE UNION
47 MARYLEBONE LANE, LONDON, W1M 6AX

By the same author:

UNDERSTANDING BASIC BELIEFS formerly TO TELL YOU THE TRUTH

UNDERSTANDING THE TEN COMMANDMENTS formerly GOD'S FRONTIERS

WHO DIED WHY

UNDERSTANDING OURSELVES formerly THE TROUBLED MIND

CHRISTIAN ANSWERS TO CONTEMPORARY PROBLEMS

CHRISTIAN ANSWERS ABOUT DOCTRINE

IT'S A GREAT LIFE

UNDERSTANDING LEADERSHIP formerly WHAT MAKES A LEADER

First published 1977

ISBN 0 85421 327 9

Printed in Great Britain at The Spottiswoode Ballantyne Press, by William Clowes & Sons Limited, London, Colchester and Beccles.

Contents

Introduction

The purpose of this book is to try to discover what the Bible teaches about some of the fundamental subjects of the Christian life; for at a time when there are so many different and conflicting ideas and opinions floating around, it is more than ever important to know what the Scriptures themselves have to say. Comment has therefore been kept as short as possible, and the Bible has been allowed to speak for itself.

It is hoped that the individual Christian using this book will find the Scriptural passages chosen a real source of encouragement and strength, and will make time to commit some of them to memory, adding in the spaces provided other verses which he discovers for himself. The different subjects with their statements and references could also form a useful basis for group Bible study and discussion. No single version of the Bible has been suggested (though all the standard ones are recommended), because it is realized that each reader will have his own favourite, and because the sense of the passages chosen does not depend significantly upon the particular translation which is used.

Many helpful books have been written on the subjects covered here, and while it is hoped that this present book will lead to a clearer understanding of the great truths of the Christian Faith, its usefulness will depend largely upon the extent to which the reader is prepared to pursue the study of these matters more deeply for himself.

July 1977 John Eddison

1. Angels

i. What are they?

They are not promoted Christians, or a kind of spiritual peerage, but a specially created order of beings, untouched by sin, who live in the immediate presence of God. They are not subject to the ordinary laws which govern human life. They are often described as white and shining, as though reflecting something of the glory of God. In no sense are they intermediaries between man and God, and worship of them is forbidden in the Bible. It is clear that at some stage certain angels rebelled against God, and were cast out of heaven, among whom was Satan.

Matt.22.30
Luke 15.10
Matt.28.2-4
Col.2.18
Rev.22.8,9
2 Pet.2.4
Luke 10.18

ii. What do they do?

a. They worship God, and praise him continually. Heb.1.6

b. They come to the help of God's people at critical and important times. How much we owe to them today, it is impossible to say, and it could be that the universal presence of the Holy Spirit has made their ministry less necessary than it was.

Psa.34.7
Gen.22.11
Luke 22.43
Acts 27.23
Heb.1.14

c. They will accompany Christ when he returns to earth in triumph, and they will have some kind of share in the judgement of men and women.

Matt.25.31
2 Thess.1.7,8
Matt.13.39,49

2. Assurance (of salvation)

i. Can we expect to be sure?

God does not want us to live in a kind of twilight of doubt, like people waiting for the result of an exam or an operation. He wants us to know, humbly but confidently, that if we have trusted Christ, our sins are forgiven.

John 5.24; John 20.30,31; 1 John 5.13; 2 Tim. 1.12

ii. On what does our assurance rest?

a. On the word of God, for in many places he has promised that those who turn to him will be accepted, and will find forgiveness and life.

Heb.10.23; Rom.4.21; John 6.37; Rev.3.20

b. On the work of Christ, because when Jesus died, he made 'a full, perfect and sufficient sacrifice . . . for the sins of the whole world'. Every debt has been paid and cancelled. 'All is finished, and nothing remains, but man's acceptance of Calvary's gains.'

John 19.30; Heb.9.11-14; 24-26; 1 John 1.7

c. On the witness of the Holy Spirit, because sooner or later he will begin to make his presence felt in the heart and life of the person who has trusted in Christ for salvation. He will give an inner certainty that we belong to Christ. He will create within us a new outlook and attitude — a hatred of sin and a new power to fight it; a love for other Christians; an enjoyment of prayer and Bible reading.

Rom.8.16; 2 Cor.5.17; 1 John 2.29; 3.9,,14 4.4; 5.4; Psa.97.10; Psa.119.97, 104; Mal.3.16

iii. Can we ever lose our salvation?

No! Once we have received Christ, we become sons of God, and we can never be 'defiliated'. A relationship comes into existence which can never be broken. But through deliberate sin we can spoil our friendship with him, and when that happens, we must ask to be forgiven. We do not lose our salvation, but we may lose the joy of it. Jesus compared us to a man who had been to the town baths. On the way back, his feet would get dusty, and so he washed them. He did not need a bath, only a rinse, and he was completely restored.

John 1.12; Gal.3.26; John 10.27,28; Heb.13.5; 1 John 1.9-2.2; Psa.51.12; John 13.3-11

3. Baptism (or christening)

i. What is the idea of this practice?

Many movements and societies have a form of initiation by which new members are enrolled. In the Old Testament circumcision was the outward sign of those who had entered a covenant or treaty with God; and in the New Testament Baptism became the visible mark of those who were willing to follow Christ and enter the Kingdom of God. Going down into the water was a sign of the washing away of sin, and coming up again a sign of a new life to be lived.

Gen.17.9-14
Rom.6.4
Col.2.12
Acts 8.36-38
Acts 9.18

ii Why are babies baptized?

This practice, which is followed by the Church of England, is felt to be a natural parallel to the Old Testament practice of circumcision, and expresses the desire of Christian parents to bring up their children in the faith. The baby is of course unconscious of what is happening, and promises are made on its behalf by sponsors or godparents. A later service of Confirmation, when it reaches a responsible age, gives the child the chance to declare its own faith in Christ, and confirm the promises made for it in infancy. Taken together, Baptism and Confirmation in the Church of England correspond to the one service of Adult Baptism practised in other churches.

Matt.19.14
Acts 16.33

iii. What is the baptism of the Holy Spirit?

Baptism in water is of no value in itself unless it is accompanied by faith in Jesus Christ. It is when we trust in him, and receive him as our Saviour, that the Holy Spirit takes up residence in our hearts, and we are said to be 'baptized of the Holy Spirit'. It is he alone who can do spiritually what the water does physically. He does inwardly what the water does outwardly, washing away our sin, and raising us to a new life in his power.

Matt.3.11
John 3.1-8
Acts 1.5; 11.16
1 Cor.12.13

4. The Bible

i. Is it reliable?

The Bible claims to be God's revelation of Himself — the Book, that is, in which he makes known his will and purpose for mankind. What evidence is there for this?

2 Tim.3.16
2 Pet.1.20,21

a. Jesus himself treated it as the 'Word of God' which could not be broken.

Matt.5.17-19
John 10.35

b. On all the great and important subjects it speaks from start to finish with one voice: God's attitude towards sin, for example, or his love for mankind, or the purpose of man's existence in the world.

Gen.3.22-24
Isa.29.1-2
Rev.21.27
Jer.31.3
John 3.16
1 John 4.10

c. Throughout history it has had a dynamic effect for good upon all who have read it humbly and thoughtfully.

Neh.8.1-8
Acts 8.26-40

d. Many attempts have been made to stamp it out, or ban it, or make the reading of it illegal, but none of these efforts have succeeded and it is still the world's best seller.

Jer.36
1 Pet.1.23-25

ii. Is it relevant?

a. It informs. We shall not expect to find up-to-date information about medicine, science and so on in the Bible, but on the all-important subject of man's relationship to God, it is our only source of knowledge.

Luke 24.25-27
John 5.39
Acts 17.2, 11; 18.24-28; 26.22,23

b. It instructs. It is only through the Bible that we can learn what is the purpose and will of God for his creatures: why we are here at all, what is expected of us, how we should behave, and so on.

2 Tim.3.16
Luke 10.26
Rom.15.4

iii. Is it readable?

a. Too difficult. The Bible is not always easy to understand, and this is where a good modern translation, Bible reading notes, books and the help of other Christians can be of great assistance.

Acts 8.29-35

b. Too dangerous. Some find the demands of the Bible too great and its challenge too strong for comfort, and prefer to put it on one side.

Jer.36
James 1.22

c. Too dull. The Bible is dull for those who have never started the Christian life. Just as a stained glass window will only 'come alive' when you enter the cathedral, and just as a map will only 'make sense' when you start to explore the country it represents, so the Bible is only of real value to those who have begun the Christian life; but then it becomes the most precious possession we have.

It is like *food,* which we not only enjoy, but which can build us up, and make us spiritually strong and healthy. Deut.8.3 Psa.19.9,10 1 Pet.2.2 Jer.15.16

It is like a *lamp* which can show us the path we ought to take, what to believe and how to behave. Psa.119.105

It is like a *sword* with which we can fight temptation, and which can pierce its way through to people's minds and consciences. Eph.6.17 Heb.4.12

It is like a *mirror,* for it points ot our faults, and shows us what needs to be corrected. James 1.22,23

5. The Church

i. What is it?

The word comes from the Greek, and means those who have been 'called out', that is, from the world, into friendship with Christ, and it is used to describe the world-wide company of Christian believers, as well as the place where they meet to worship. Mark 3.14

a. It is like a **body.** Christ being the Head of that body, and the individual members being the limbs and other organs; and through this body Christ is active in the world today. Eph.1.22, 23 1 Cor.12.12-31 Col.1.18

b. It is like a **building,** the foundation stone being Christ himself, each brick being an individual Christian, and the occupier of the building being the Holy Spirit. Eph.2.19-22 1 Cor.3.16 1 Pet.2.5

c. It is like a **family,** of which Christ is the Head, and Christians are the brothers and sisters. Eph.3.14,15

d. It is like a **bride,** united to Christ in faithfulness and love. Eph.5.22-27

e. It is like an **army,** engaged in continuous war against the powers of evil in the world. Eph.6.11,12 1 Pet.5.8,9

ii. What is its function in the world?

All these different metaphors suggest different tasks which the Church must perform, but perhaps it has two principal activities.

a. To worship — that is, to offer up to God praise, thanksgiving and prayer. 1 Pet.2.5 Mal.1.11

b. To witness — that is, to show forth the love and power of God to the world around. 1 Pet.2.9

6. Communion

i. What is it?

The original 'Lord's Supper' in the upper room was part of the annual Jewish Passover Feast. Later on it probably became an informal meal at which Christians enjoyed each other's company, and then at some point broke bread and drank wine to commemorate the death of Jesus. We are familiar with the 'Loyal Toast' which is drunk at the end of dinners, and it could perhaps have been almost as simple as that. Later still it seems that the feast sometimes became an occasion for greed and selfishness, and that Paul may have encouraged the Christians to hold the commemorative part of it separately, and thus we have the beginnings of the distinctive service of Holy Communion as we know it today. Matt.26.26-31 Acts 2.42 1 Cor.11.17-22, 33, 34

ii. What does it signify?

a. It is an act of **fellowship,** or *communion* between Christians who are sharing the same loaf and drinking from the same cup. 1 Cor.10.16,17 1 Cor.11.20-22

b. It is an act of **witness** by which we show to the outside world the tremendous importance we attach to the death of Jesus. 1 Cor.11.26

c. It is an act of **remembrance,** as we call to mind what Christ did for us upon the cross. 1 Cor.11.23-25

d. It is an act of **identification** with him, for while we eat the bread and drink the wine, we may 'feed on him in our hearts by faith with thanksgiving.' 1 Cor.11.27-29

7. Conscience

i. What is conscience?

A kind of moral barometer or compass: a God-given way of distinguishing good from evil and right from wrong.

John 8.9
Rom.2.15
Rom.9.1

ii. Is it infallible?

Unfortunately not, because it has become dislocated or twisted by sin. It is like a compass that is incapable of indicating the true north, or a clock that refuses to keep proper time; and many evil things have been done by people who have claimed to have had 'a perfectly clear conscience'. It can be muffled too, by the noise and excitement of life, rather like the alarm clock we bury under a pile of clothes. But in most people it is not wholly inaccurate, and more or less awake.

1 Tim.4.2
Titus 1.15

iii. What should we do about it?

a. It needs **cleaning.** Like our hearts and minds, it has become contaminated with sin.

b. It needs **regulating.** If it is to be of any real use to us, we must 'set it' by God's standards, so that it will tell us at once when we swerve from what he has told us is right and good.

Heb.9.14
Heb.10.2
Heb.13.18
Acts 23.1
Acts 24.16
1 Tim.1.5,19
1 Tim.3.9
1 Pet.3.21

8. Conversion

i. What does the word mean?

It doesn't occur very often in the Bible, but it is a word which conveniently describes the act by which a sinner turns to God for forgiveness.

Psa.51.13
Luke 22.32
Acts 3.19
James 5.19

ii. How are we converted?

There are usually five distinct aspects of true conversion.

a. A sense of need. That is, a readiness to admit that we are sinners who deserve God's punishment.

Rom.3.22,23
Rom.6.23

b. An understanding of the cross. We can never fully grasp its meaning, but we need to know that, 'He died that we might be forgiven'.

John 1.29
John 3.16
Rom.5.8
1 Pet.3.18

c. A willingness to turn from sin. This is what the Bible calls 'repentance' (q.v.). God can only forgive what we are willing to forsake.

Isa.55.7
Acts 26.18
1 Thess.1.9

d. A counting of the cost. We must be prepared to be known as Christ's disciples, and, 'manfully to fight under his banner'.

Luke 9.23-27
Luke 9.57-62

e. A committal of ourselves to him. The Bible describes this last step in several different ways. It speaks of 'coming to Christ', or 'receiving him', or 'following him'. They all add up to the same idea — a personal encounter and surrender to Christ.

Matt.11.28
Rev.3.20
John 1.12
Matt.4.18-22

9. The Cross

i. What was so special about the death of Jesus?

a. It was **voluntary.** He need not have died. He could have hidden from the Jews, escaped from the soldiers and come down from the cross. But he chose to die, and deliberately 'gave his life'.

John 10.17,18
1 Pet.2.23
Isa.53.7-9

b. It was **innocent.** No one could find any fault with him. The people who watched him and heard him critically, his sworn enemies, his chosen friends — they all came to the same conclusion: he was 'without sin'.

John 8.46
Matt.27.24
Luke 23.4,41,47
1 Pet.2.21,22
2 Cor.5.21
1 John 3.5
Heb.4.15

c. It was **sacrificial.** He died for others, on their behalf; and his death did for them something they could not do for themselves.

John 10.11,15
Isa.53.5

d. It was **victorious.** Death was unable to keep him in its grasp, and he rose again from the grave.

Acts 2.24
Acts 26.23
1 Cor.15.20

ii. What did his death achieve for us?

a. It redeemed us from sin. We were like prisoners, kidnapped by sin, for whom a ransom had to be provided; and Christ in his love 'gave his life a ransom' for us.

Mark 10.45
Ep.1.7
1 Tim.2.6
Titus 2.14
1 Pet.1.18,19

b. It reconciled us to God. We were not just prisoners, we were enemies, because we had rebelled against God. We deserved to be punished, but Jesus took our place, bore the punishment instead of us, that he might make peace between us and God, and restore us to a state of friendship with him. He did more, for he 'justified' us in God's sight. Because Christ died for us, we are not just 'let off', nor even simply 'taken back' we are *'made right',* or legally acquitted. The verdict has not just been 'quashed'; it has been 'reversed'.

Isa.53.4-6
Acts 13.39
Rom.5.8,9
2 Cor.5.19
Col.1.21
1 Tim.2.5
1 Pet.3.18

10. Death

i. What is meant by death in the Bible?

The Bible distinguishes between three kinds of death.

a. Physical death. This kind of death is the experience of every living creature, and the Bible makes it clear that it is the direct result of the fact that sin has come into the world.

Gen.2.16,17
Rom.5.12
1 Cor.15.21,22

b. Spiritual death. There is a sense in which everyone is 'born dead', because ordinary human beings are unaware of the existence of spiritual things. By nature we are, so to speak, 'tone deaf' or 'colour blind' where the things of God are concerned. We need to be born again.

Rom.8.6
Eph.2.1,5
Col.2.12

c. Eternal death. Sin is rebellion against God, and he must punish it by banishing the sinner from himself. To be banished or separated from him in this way is to suffer eternal death.

Isa.59.1,2
Rom.6.23

ii. Is there any possible escape from death?

There is — through Christ.

a. Because He died upon the cross, our sins may be forgiven, the cause of separation can be removed, and we can enjoy 'eternal life'.

John 3.14-16
John 5.24
Rom.5.21
Rom.6.23

b. Because He rose from the dead and lives for evermore, we know that death has been finally conquered, and that we too will rise again to live a new kind of life in a new body which God will prepare for us.

1 Cor.15
Heb.2.14,15

c. Because He lives today, He can come into my heart and life and bring about within me the miracle of a new birth, and so I become 'alive unto God'.

John 1.12
John 3.3,5
Rom.6.13
1 Pet.1.3-5

11. The Devil

i. Is there a personal Devil?

The Bible always speaks of the Devil as if he was a real person, and we know that Jesus encountered him. Moreover, as we look around us it is not difficult to see evidence of his presence and his power, or to believe that 'the Prince of this world', as Jesus called him, exercises widespread control over the hearts and minds of people.

Job 1.6-12
Matt.4.1-11
John 14.30
1 John 5.19

ii. Who is he?

This we cannot say for certain, but there are hints in the Bible that he may once have been an angel (q.v.) who set himself up against God, and was thrown out of heaven.

Job 4.18
Isa.14.12-17
Luke 10.18

iii. What does he do?

He is known as 'Satan', which means the 'Adversary', and it is his function to oppose the will of God in every possible way, and to promote evil throughout the world. He tries to blind people to the truth of the gospel, and if he fails in this attempt, then he does his best to entice them away from Christ. Everything that is wrong with the world may be traced back to his malevolent influence — and 'Ever to do ill' is 'his sole delight'.

Gen.3.1
Luke 13.16
Luke 22.31
2 Cor.4.3,4
2 Cor.11.14
Eph.6.11
1 Thess.2.18
1 Pet.5.8

iv. What will happen to him?

Through his death and resurrection, Jesus dealt Satan a mortal blow from which he can never recover. The war against him has been won, but it is not yet over his final overthrow and destruction will follow the return of Christ, and the setting up of his kingdom.

Gen.3.15
Matt.25.41
Rom.16.20
2 Pet.2.4
Rev.12.9
Rev.20.10

12. Discipleship

i. What is a disciple?

Perhaps our nearest equivalent word is 'apprentice', that is, someone who learns from a master craftsman by listening, watching and questioning. For these reasons it is a word applied to a follower of Jesus.

Mark 3.14
Mark 4.34
John 21.14

ii. What are the qualifications for a disciple?

a. Faith. We must have confidence in the one who is teaching and leading us. John 2.11

b. Obedience. If we are to make any progress, there must be a willingness to carry out his instructions. John 8.31

c. Love. The closer the disciples are to their Master, the closer they will be drawn to each other in caring, Christian love. John 13.35

d. Fruitfulness. The Master has every right to expect his character and qualities to be reproduced in the lives of his disciples. John 15.8

e. Suffering. The disciple must expect the same sort of treatment which his Master had to endure; and because Jesus met with mockery and hostility, we must be prepared for that too. Matt.10.24

13. Faith

i. What is faith?

It is belief founded upon authority — not just belief in anything (that is credulity), but belief for which there are solid and sensible reasons. In the case of Christianity it is basically belief in the existence of a God who is altogether wise, powerful and loving; and in Jesus Christ as his divine son.

Luke 1.1-4
Rom.1.19-21
Heb.11.1

ii. How do we get faith?

a. It comes from what we **learn** *about God from the Bible* — what he has done for others and what he can do for us; just as our faith in a doctor or music teacher stems from what we learn from other people about his character and ability. Rom.10.17 1 Thess.2.13

b. It grows by **experience,** for the more we put him to the test, the more trustworthy we find him to be. Psa.34.8 Rom.5.3-5 John 4.39-42

iii. Why is faith so important?

a. Because without it we cannot please God. Not to trust him when we have every reason to do so is like a vote of no confidence in him. Heb.11.6 Luke 18.8

b. Because faith is like a 'master key'. It opens nearly all the doors of Christian experience.

It is by faith that we find forgiveness and salvation. John 3.16 Eph.2.5-8

It is the secret of victory over temptation. 1 Pet.5.5 1 John 5.4

It is a necessary condition for having our prayers answered. Matt.21.22 James 1.5

It is one of the most important secrets of progress in the Christian life. 2 Cor.5.7 1 Tim.1.19

14. God

i. Does he exist?

We cannot prove the existence of God mathematically, but rather in the same sort of way as people are proved innocent or guilty in a court of law, that is to say, by the weight of evidence for or against. What sort of evidence is there?

a. The universe as we know it can only be satisfactorily explained if we admit the existence of a Cause of unlimited power and wisdom. Psa.19.1,2 Rom.1.19,20

b. In human beings all over the world there is a deeply rooted instinct to worship and serve something beyond themselves. Must there not therefore be a means for satisfying it, as there is for satisfying other instincts like thirst and sex? Acts 17.22-31 John 4.22

c. The Bible claims to be the record of God's dealings with his creatures, and millions of people throughout history would assert that through it they came to experience his love and power in their lives.

2 Pet.1.21
Heb.1.1
2 Tim.3.16

d. Jesus Christ claimed to be God in human form, and he supported that claim, which would otherwise have been preposterous, by his teaching, his sinless character, the miracles of his birth and resurrection, as well as the many miracles which he himself performed.

John 1.1-14; 14.9
Col.2.9
Heb.1.2-4

ii. What is he like?

a. He is a **spiritual** *being.* That is to say, he does not need, as we do, a physical body in order to express himself or execute his will in the world.

Deut.4.15
Isa.40.18-27
John 4.24
Acts 17.29

b. He is an **eternal** *being.* That is, he lives outside as well as within our framework of time and space, rather as an author lives outside (and at the same time inside) the book he has written.

Isa.57.15
Hab.1.12

c. He is a **moral** *being.* In other words, he is infinitely holy and righteous, and utterly opposed to sin in every shape and form. This holiness is expressed in the Bible in such metaphorical terms as 'snow', 'fire', 'light'.

Psa.11.7
Isa.33.14
Hab.1.13
1 Tim.6.16
1 John 1.5

d. He is a **personal** *being.* He is never described in the Bible as an impersonal, mechanical force, but always in personal terms, as Creator, Father, Judge — one who deals with his creatures as people and not as machines.

Isa.40.28
Psa.103.13
Mal.3.17
Gen.18.25
Psa.96.13

iii. Can he be known?

We can learn a great deal about a famous person by visiting the house where he lives, reading the books that he wrote, talking perhaps to people who knew him. In the same way nature, the Church, the Bible and other people can teach us a tremendous lot about God; but after all their efforts we can still find ourselves saying, 'I wish I knew him for myself'. But through Jesus Christ we can actually be introduced to God, and come to know him personally. To receive Christ into our hearts is to begin a personal friendship with God.

John 17.3
Gal.4.6
Phil.3.10
1 John 5.12
Rev.3.20

15. Guidance

i. Does God really guide people?

He promises to do so, and there are many occasions in the Bible on which he intervened to show men and women what they ought to do and how they ought to behave. Psa.48.14 Isa.58.11

ii. How does he guide people?

In the Old Testament, and quite often in the New Testament too, he used things like dreams, visitations and visions to show people what they should do. Gradually, it would seem, these have given way to rather less direct methods. Ex.13.20-22 Matt.2.13,19,20

a. Chiefly, of course, he guides us through the *Bible*, and it can never be right to go against what is specifically laid down there. Josh.1.8 Psa.119.105 2 Tim.3.16

b. Conscience (q.v.), if tuned as it must be to the Bible, will nearly always enable us to distinguish right from wrong. Isa.30.21 Acts 24.16 Rom.2.15 1 Tim.1.19

c. The advice of Christian friends who know us well, though not infallible, can be of very great help. Acts 15.25-29

d. If we believe that God is in complete control of affairs, then he will often indicate his will to us by the way in which he arranges the *circumstances* of our lives. Gen.24.27 Gen.50.20 Rom.8.28

iii. Are there any conditions for being guided?

a. We must be *humble* and submissive, and willing to go God's way whatever it may cost. Psa.32.8,9 John 7.17

b. We must be *trusting*, and believe that he will reveal his will to us, even though he may not do so immediately or all at once. Prov.3.5-7

16. Heaven

i. Where is it?

The Bible does not tell us where heaven is, but it leaves us in no doubt that it is a definite place, and not just a state of mind. It is the dwelling-place of God, and the place from which Christ came and to which he returned.

Deut.26.15
Psa.11.4
Psa.33.13,14
Luke 11.2
John 3.13
John 6.33
Acts 1.11
Heb.9.24

ii. What is it like?

We have poetical descriptions of it in many parts of the Bible, notably in the Book of Revelation. Perhaps the most important thing to say about it is that it is the place where God is, and from which everything is excluded which has spoiled life on earth — sin, suffering, sorrow and evil in every shape and form. The chief occupation of those who live there is the worship and the service of God.

Rev.7.9-17
Rev.21

iii. Who will go there?

All who have trusted in Christ, whose sins have been forgiven and who have been born again into the Kingdom of Heaven, are qualified to enter.

Psa.24.3-6
John 3.3
John 14.2,3
1 Pet.1.3-5

17. Hell

i. Where is it?

As in the case of Heaven, the Bible gives us no clue as to its whereabouts. The fact that it is always thought of as 'down there' and Heaven as 'up there' is probably just an appropriate figure of speech; but there is no doubt that Christ meant us to think of it as a real place, as he did with Heaven (q.v). (NB When the Apostles' Creed speaks of Jesus as having 'descended into hell', a different word is used, and a better phrase would be 'the resting-place of the dead'.)

Psa.9.17
Mark 9.43,44

ii. What will it be like?

Once again, if we look behind the imagery which the Bible uses, two facts stand out: it will be a *place of separation* (where God is not), and a *place of suffering.*

Luke 16.19-31

iii. Who will go there?

We are told that it is the place reserved for those who in heart and life reject the claims of Christ, and expose themselves to His judgement and condemnation.

John 3.18
2 Thess.1.7-9

18. The Holy Spirit

i. Who or what is he?

He is not an influence or an atmosphere, but a Person — the third Person of what is called the Trinity. We don't read very much about him in the Old Testament, though he was actively present, and we find him associated with God's work of creation, equipping God's servants for special work and inspiring the prophets. On the Day of Pentecost, after Jesus' return to heaven, he was poured out in a new way upon all Christian believers.

2 Cor.14.13
Gen.1.2
Gen.2.7
Psa.104.30
Psa.139.7-10
Jud.6.34
2 Pet.1.21
Acts 2.1-4

ii. What is his work?

a. He is an **ambassador.** He represents Christ, and takes the place of Christ in the heart of the individual Christian believer. He makes Christ real to us, and reminds us of his teaching.

John 14.17,26
John 15.26
John 16.7,14.

b. He is a **benefactor.** He bestows upon Christians the gifts they need for serving Christ, equipping them with power to witness for him, and producing in them the 'fruit of the Spirit,' as it is called: 'love, joy, peace ...'

Acts 1.8
1 Cor.12 & 14
Gal.5.22,23

c. He is a **counsellor.** He guides us when we are perplexed, and don't quite know what to believe or how to behave, and he reproduces in us the mind of Christ. He helps us in our prayers and when we are tempted, stimulates us when we are lazy, and comforts us when we are sad.

John 16.13
Rom.8.26
Eph.3.16

iii. How do we receive him?

When we 'receive Christ' as our Saviour, and invite him into our hearts, it is the Holy Spirit who actually takes up residence there, making us his dwelling-place and headquarters.

John 14.16-18
Rev.3.20
1 Cor.3.16
1 Cor.6.19

19. Jesus Christ

i. Who was he?

a. Son of God. Jesus was not just a very good man who was promoted to be God. He was God from the very start — God seen in human form. Just as light becomes visible when it is passed through a prism and broken up into the colours of the rainbow, so Jesus, 'the light of the world', showed us what God was really like. He made God visible, audible. The 'Thought' (God) became the 'Word' (Jesus); the 'Author' became the 'Actor', taking the part of one of his own characters. What proof have we of this?

John 1.14,18
Col.1.19; 2.9
1 Tim.3.16
Heb.1.1-3
1 John 1.1

There was first of all his *miraculous birth,* for while he had a human mother, Jesus had no human father.

Matt.1.18-25

Next there was his *sinless life,* for no one was able to find fault with anything he said or did.

John 8.46
2 Cor.5.21
Heb.4.15

There were also his *claims* to have come direct from God which, if they were not true, meant that he was either a freak or a fraud.

John 6.33-35
John 11.25
John 14.6,9,20
John 17.21

And these claims were supported by the many *miracles* which he performed, the like of which have never been seen, before or since.

John 3.2
John 10.37,38
John 15.24

Finally, there was the greatest miracle of all, his own *resurrection* from the dead (q.v).

Acts 2.23,24
Rom1.3,4

b. Son of Man. Jesus was not God masquerading as man, like someone wearing a disguise. He really did become man. Like the 'live' rail, he was the same in appearance as the others, but charged with unique divine power and grace.

Physically he was man, and knew what it was to be hungry, thirsty and sleepy, and to suffer pain.

Matt.4.2
John 19.28
Mark 4.38

Emotionally he was man, and experienced joy and sorrow.

John 15.11
John 11.35

Morally he was man, and knew the full force of temptation.

Heb.2.10,18
Heb.4.15

ii. Why did He come?

There were many important by-products of Jesus coming — many things which would not have happened if he had never come.

a. For the first time people saw what God was really like. John 14.9

b. The Old Testament Scriptures were illuminated in a new way, and the Law and the Prophets, only sketched in outline before, were 'fulfilled' and given their complete meaning. Luke 24.25-27 Matt.5.17,18

c. Many who were sick, disabled and handicapped found new life and hope and health through the ministry of Jesus. Matt.11.4,5 Luke 4.18,19

d. But all these were subsidiary to the main purpose of his coming which was to mount the biggest rescue operation in history — the salvation of mankind from sin and death, and this supreme work he could only do through his own death upon the cross. Matt.1.21 Mark 10.45 Luke 19.10 John 3.14-17 John 12.27-33 1 John 4.14

iii. Where is he now?

At his ascension, Jesus returned to his Father's presence where he represents Christian believers as their advocate and ambassador. God now deals with us through Christ, and on the strength of his death and resurrection. Acts 7.56 Heb.1.3 Heb.7.25 Heb.9.24 1 John 2.1,2

iv. Will he return?

In many places in the Bible it is clearly stated that Jesus will come back again. Last time he came to save, next time it will be to judge; last time he came to redeem, next time it will be to reign. Luke 21.25-28 John 14.3 Acts 1.11 Acts 17.31 Rev.11.15

20. Judgement

i. When will this take place?

It seems to be quite clear from the Bible that God has already appointed the day on which he will judge the world.

Acts 17.31
Rom.2.16; 14.10
2 Cor.5.10
Heb.9.27

ii. Who will be the Judge?

Sometimes God himself is spoken of as the Judge and sometimes this task seems to have been entrusted to Christ.

Psa.9.8
Acts 10.42
2 Tim.4.8
Heb.12.23

iii. On what basis will we be judged?

a. It seems that those who have never heard of Christ will be judged according to the way in which they have lived up to the Law of Moses or the light of their own conscience.

Eccles.12.14
Rom.1.20; 2.6-15
Rev.20.11,12

b. Those who have heard of Christ, and have had the chance of believing in him, will be judged according to their attitude towards him.

Matt.10.32,33; 11.21-24
John 3.16.16-18; 5.24

iv. What about the Christian believer?

While his eternal salvation will not be in question, his reward, probably in the form of further and greater responsibility in the next life, will depend upon the way in which he has lived for Christ on earth, and used the talents, time and opportunities which God has given him.

Dan.12.3
Matt.25.14-30
1 Cor.3.11-15

21. Man

i. What is man?

Physically, of course, man resembles the animals, Psa.49.12,20
and 'is like the beasts that perish', but the Bible Eccles.3.19
makes it clear that in two important respects he is unique.

a. He is made **like God.** This does not mean that Gen.1.26-28
there is any physical or outward resemblance, but Gen.5.1
that, like God, man possesses a mind, a conscience Gen.9.6
and a will. He has the power to reason, to make James 3.9
moral distinctions, and to choose.

b. He is made **for God.** He has been created with Psa.8.4-8
what has been called 'a God-shaped cavity', which Isa.43.7,21
means that he only finds true satisfaction in life if he is in fellowship with his Maker, worshipping and serving him, partly by cultivating the world in which God has placed him.

ii. What has gone wrong with man?

Man has declared his independence from God, Gen.3.22-24
rebelled against him and disobeyed his Isa.53.6
commands. Instead of living for his Maker, he has Rom.3.9-18,23
chosen a life of selfishness and sin. The original image is still there, but, like the sovereign's head on a very old coin, it is in many cases almost indiscernible.

iii. Can man be put right?

Yes. This has been God's purpose from the earliest 2 Chron.36.14-16
days, and it is what the Law and the Prophets tried Dan.9.9,10
but failed to do. It has finally been achieved in two 2 Pet.3.9
ways.

a. Jesus, through his death on the cross (q.v) Eph.2.13,14
reconciled us to God: ended the state of war Col.1.20,21
between us, and made peace.

b. The Holy Spirit, by living in our hearts and Rom.8.29
lives, can *restore* the image which sin has 2 Cor.3.18
damaged, so that gradually we may become more Col.3.10
and more Christ-like.

22. Marriage

i. What is the point of marriage?

a. Human beings were not intended to live alone, and God made men and women in such a way that they should perfectly complement each other. 'What the fork is to the knife, that the man is to his wife.' And marriage was ordained 'for the mutual society, help, and comfort, that the one ought to have of the other, both in prosperity and adversity'. Gen.2.18 Eccles.4.9-12

b. Marriage is the way God has chosen for bringing children into the world and providing them with a stable home background. Gen.1.26-28 Gen.9.1 Eph.6.1-3

c. It is also the way in which the sex instinct which he has implanted can be directed according to his will and used to his glory. Gen.2.23,24 Eph.5.31

ii. What sort of a relationship ought marriage to be?

a. A lasting one. This is obvious if marriage involves, as it does, the setting up of a new home in which children can be brought up in security and happiness. Matt.19.5,6

b. A loving one. Love will show itself in different ways, some more obviously masculine and some feminine; but in every truly Christian marriage we shall find reverence and honour, protection and care, humility and submission. Eph.5.22-33 Col.3.18,19 1 Pet.3.1-7

iii. Does that mean that divorce is wrong?

Divorce in the Bible is always regarded as a last resort, only to be entertained if every possible remedy has been tried and failed, and a marriage has reached a point of irretrievable breakdown. Mal.2.16 Matt.19.3-9

23. Miracles

i. Can we really believe in them?

a. If we believe in a Creator-God, then we have to start by admitting that the very fact of life itself is a miracle; and it is perfectly reasonable to suppose that the Maker can intervene when he wants to do so, to alter the time-table, or to change the course of events in his own creation.

Gen.18.14
Jer.32.17
Zech.8.6
Matt.19.26
Luke 1.37

b. The resurrection (q.v.) of Jesus from the dead has been called the 'grand miracle' — the evidence for which is perhaps stronger than for any other miracle — and if God could perform this, then surely he can do anything, and the others seem almost trivial by comparison.

Acts 2.32
Acts 3.15
Acts 4.10
Acts 10.40
Eph.1.19,20

c. It is possible that there are 'natural' explanations of some miracles, but this does not alter or affect the miraculous element in their foretelling or timing.

Ex.10.10-20
Ex.14.21

ii. Why were they necessary?

a. They demonstrated God's power, and showed all who saw them who really was in control of events.

Psa.72.18
Psa.136.4
Psa.145.3-6

b. They were always performed for the benefit of certain people or nations.

Psa.107

c. They strengthened the faith and confidence of God's people in himself — e.g. the plagues in Egypt gradually prepared the children of Israel to trust God for the exodus.

Ex.14.31
John 2.11

d. On many occasions they taught some inner lesson, and were a kind of acted parable.

John 2.11
John 3,5
John 6.5-13,35
John 11.23-27

iii. Why don't they happen today?

It would be quite wrong to assume that they don't. Prayers are answered, God's providence is at work, and many people testify to happenings which seem to move at right angles to the ordinary course of events. But if they do not happen as they did in Bible days, it could be for one of two reasons. It

John 14.12
Mark 16.17,18
Rom.8.28
Matt.13.58
John 20.29
2 Cor.5.7
1 Pet.1.8

might be due to lack of faith on the part of Christian people today; or it could be that in the fullest sense the age of miracles has passed, and that God has wanted to wean his people away from too great a dependence upon their senses, and to teach them to walk by faith and not by sight.

24. Money

i. Is there anything wrong in possessing it?

The Bible does not comdemn the possession of money as such, and seems rather to accept the existence of rich and poor as a fact of life; but it has a lot to say about certain attitudes towards money which it regards as dangerous and even positively sinful.

Eccles.5.19
Prov.21.20;
22.1-4

ii. What are wrong attitudes to money?

a. Craving it. Some people will do almost anything to get money, and the Bible condemns utterly every dishonest method of acquiring it: stealing, corruption, sharp practice, extortion, usury.

Prov.20.10,23
23.4,5
James 5.3,4
Jer.17.11
Hos.12.7,8
Amos 8.4-7

b. Loving it. The love of money can steal the loyalty and love we owe to Christ, and can very easily lead us into sinful methods of getting it.

Matt.19.16-26
1 Tim.6.6-10
James 5.1-3
Heb.13.5

c. Trusting it. The Bible warns us not to trust in the uncertainty of riches which we cannot take with us when we die. They are a false security.

Psa.52.7
Psa.62.10
Prov.11.28;
27.24

d. Hoarding it. If money is a gift from God, then it matters very much how we use it — not selfishly, but generously and wisely.

Jer.9.23
Luke 12.15-21
1 Tim.6.17
1 Tim.6.18

e. Vaunting it. The possession of money can make people proud and arrogant, and encourage them to adopt extravagant habits.

1 John 3.17
James 2.1-7

25. The New Birth

i. What is meant by the 'new birth'?

It is the New Testament way of describing what happens to a person when he becomes a true follower of Jesus Christ. He is given a new life to live, a new nature, new tastes, desires and inclinations.

2 Cor.5.17
Rom.6.4
Gal.6.15

ii. Why is it necessary?

a. In order to enter God's **kingdom.** A new birth would be necessary if a plant were to become an animal, or an animal a man; and in the same way men and women can only enter the highest of all the 'kingdoms', the Kingdom of God, by being born again.

John 3.1-13

b. In order to enter God's **family.** There is a sense in which all men are 'the offspring of God' by virtue of the fact that he created us, but we are described in the Bible as being by nature 'children of disobedience' and 'children of wrath', and if we are to enter God's family in any meaningful sense we need to be born again.

2 Cor.6.17,18
Eph.1.5
Eph.2.2,3,18,19

iii. How does this new birth take place?

It is a miracle which God operates within us when we put our trust in Christ, and receive him into our hearts as our Saviour and Lord.

John 1.12,13
Gal.3.26

26. The Occult

i. What is meant by this word?

Literally it means 'that which is kept secret', and which lies beyond the range of human knowledge. Some people try to penetrate this veil, but the Christian must be prepared humbly to accept the fact there are mysteries which God means at present to keep hidden from us, and that to attempt to probe them is to go outside his will.

Job 5.8,9; 11.7
Isa.55.8,9
Rom.11.33-36

ii. What form do these practices take?

a. Communication with the dead, or necromancy, as it is called. It is clear that this practice, with its accompanying apparatus of seances and mediums, is forbidden and condemned throughout the Bible.

Lev.19.31; 20,6
1 Sam.28.7-20
1 Chron.10.13,14
Isa.8.19,20

b. Visitations from the dead in the form of ghosts, poltergeists and so on. Beyond admitting that there was a general belief in these things, Scripture is silent on this subject. As these phenomena are usually unsought, no blame can be attached to those who experience them.

Matt.14.26
Luke 24.36-39

c. Divinations. There is of course a good sense in which this word is used when applied to the Old Testament prophets to whom God gave special instructions concerning the future; but what the Bible *does* condemn is any attempt to use enchantments or other methods in order to discover the hidden purposes of God.

Deut.18.17-22
1 Sam.9.6-10
Lev.19.26
2 Kings 17.
16-18
2 Kings 21.6

27. Personal Relationships

i. What do these involve?

a. Our relations. The Bible has a lot to say about the duties of children to parents, parents to children, and husbands and wives to each other.

Ex.20.12
Prov.1.8,9
Prov.10.1
Prov.23.22-25
Col.3.20
Eph.6.4
2 Cor.12.14
Eph.5.22-33
1 Pet.3.7

b. Our neighbours. These are not just the people who live next door ('next door neighbours'), but all the people with whom we come into touch in the course of daily life.

Ex.20.13-27
Lev.19.13
Deut.19.14
Luke 10.29-37

c. Our friends. Most people have a wide circle of acquaintances, but the Christian will reserve his closest friendships for those who share his own faith. This will be particularly true when he forms business partnerships, and above all when he thinks of marriage.

Job 42.10
Prov.17.17
Prov.18.24
Prov.27.6,14
John 15.13
2 Cor.6.14,15

d. Our strangers. The Bible frequently emphasizes the Christian duty of making strangers feel welcome and at home.

Matt.25.38,43
Heb.13.2

e. Our enemies. One of the most distinctive features of Christian teaching is that we should treat our enemies as if they were our friends.

Job 31.29,30
Prov.24.17
Matt.5.43,44
Rom.12.14,20

f. Our authorities. In normal times we are called upon to submit to authority, to pay taxes and to obey laws. There may be times, when a country's leaders are inspired by anti-Christian ideas, it is necessary to protest and even to resist. There are instances of this in the Bible, but it is doubtful if there are any where passive resistance degenerated into violence.

Rom.13.1,2
1 Pet.2.13,14
Matt.22.21
Ex.1.15-17
Dan.3.18
Acts 5.27-29

ii. Is there a special relationship between Christians?

Yes, there is, and the word 'agape' had to be introduced into the vocabulary to describe the kind of love which binds Christians together, and shows itself in service, humility, kindness and sacrifice.

John 13.14,15, 34,35
1 Cor.13
Gal.6.10
1 John 3.14

28. Prayer

i. What is prayer?

It is more than just taking a shopping-list along to God, full of requests for ourselves and others. It is sharing our lives with him, and it includes praise, thanksgiving and confession as well as petition.

Psa.51
Psa.103
Luke 17.11-19
Phil.4.6
1 John 1.9

ii. Why should we ask God for things if he knows our needs already?

Asking is a way of showing that we really do want something ('those that don't ask, don't want'); and it is also a way of expressing our dependence upon him, and our humble recognition of his power to supply our needs.

Luke 11.1-13

iii. But why are some requests apparently unanswered?

Because a request is not granted, it doesn't mean that a prayer is unanswered. God may be trying to say to us, 'No', or perhaps, 'Wait'. But there are reasons why he does not answer some of our prayers as we would wish.

a. For some reason best known to him, he may not think the thing we have asked for is good for us.

Matt.20.20-23
2 Cor.12.9

b. We may have asked for something for purely selfish or unworthy motives.

James 4.1-3

c. We may have lacked the necessary faith.

James 1.5

d. We may be holding on to something sinful in our lives which prevents him from hearing us.

Psa.66.18
Isa.59.1,2

iv. When should we pray?

We can pray at any time and in any place and for any length of time; but it is also helpful to have regular times of quiet alone with God each day.

Neh.2.1-5
Isa.37.14-20
Jonah 2.1
Matt.14.28-31
Psa.55.17
Psa.5.3
Dan.6.10
1 Thess.5.17,18

29. Prophets

i. What did the prophets do?

a. Proclamation. They were the men and women through whom God spoke to the nation, often rebuking people for their wrong-doing, and warning them of his judgement to come.

Isa.6.1-8
2 Pet.1.20,21

b. Prediction. They were also inspired by God to foretell the future. Much of what they said can have meant very little to them or to their hearers at the time, but its truth became apparent in later years. This particularly applies to the many prophecies which pointed forward hundreds of years to the coming and the work of the Messiah, Jesus Christ.

1 Pet.1.10-12
Isa.53
Psa.22

ii. Are there still prophets today?

Prophecy was certainly one of the gifts which the Holy Spirit bestowed upon some of the early Christians, and in Paul's view it was an important and valuable gift. It seems, though, to have changed gradually from being the gift of foresight to one of insight — that is to say, a special understanding of God's Word, and the ability to apply it to the contemporary scene.

1 Cor.12.28
1 Cor.14.1-3

30. Repentance

i. What does this word mean?

It comes from a Greek word meaning 'a change of mind', and is nearly always used in the Bible to describe someone who has done a complete U-turn as far as sin is concerned; turning his back upon it, and determining with God's help to go in exactly the opposite direction.

Matt.3.7-12
Matt.9.13
Luke 15.17
2 Pet.3.9

ii. Why is it necessary?

For the simple reason that God cannot forgive what we are not prepared to forsake. We have got to drop the sin we are holding on to before we can take the salvation he is offering to us.

Isa.55.7
Acts 5.31
Acts 20.21

iii. Why do we read of God repenting?

It doesn't mean that God changed his mind, but rather that a change in the attitude of people towards him enabled him to act in a different way. (The sun that hardens the clay will melt the wax, for instance).

Jer.18.8

31. Resurrection

i. Did it really happen?

There seems to be overwhelming evidence that on the third day Jesus rose again from the grave.

a. When the friends of Jesus came to the tomb in the early morning, they found the huge stone rolled away, the grave — clothes apparently undisturbed, and the body of Jesus missing.

Matt.28.1-8
Luke 24.2,3
John 20.1-10

b. His friends could not have removed it (as the authorities pretended) because the tomb was very carefully guarded by Roman soldiers. In any case, why would they have wanted to do so?

Matt.27.62-66

c. The Jewish and Roman authorities had no reason for removing the body, but even if they had done so why did they not produce it and so demolish the theory of a resurrection instead of bribing the soldiers to say that the disciples had taken it?

Matt.28.11-15

d. Many people claimed to have met Jesus during the next forty days, either singly, in groups, or in a crowd.

1 Cor.15.3-8
Acts 1.1-3
Acts 10.40,41
2 Pet.1.16

e. If Jesus was not alive, how do we account for the change in the disciples? What transformed a demoralised rabble into an army which turned the world upside down?

Matt.26.56,75
Acts 4.13-22; 31-33
Acts 17.6

f. The amazing growth of the early Church could hardly have taken place if it had all been founded upon an unintentional mistake or a deliberate lie.

Rom.1.8; 16.19
1 Thess.1.8

g. Jesus himself, and the writers in the Old Testament, had foretold the fact that he would rise from the dead.

Psa.16.9,10
Isa.9.6
Isa.53.10-12
Mic.5.2
Matt.17.22,23
Luke 24.25,26, 44

ii. What difference does the resurrection of Jesus make to us?

a. Because he rose from the dead, it means that we shall also do so, and that death is not the end, but merely marks the horizon of our present earthly existence.

John 11.25,26
1 Cor.15.19-26
1 John 5.12

b. It proves that the sacrifice made by Jesus on the cross for our sins was accepted by God and completely effective.

Rom.4.25
1 Cor.15.17
1 Pet.1.18-21

c. Because he has conquered sin and Satan, we are on the winning side, and he is able to give us the victory over every temptation.

Gen.3.15
1 Cor.15.54-58

d. It means that we have a living companion who can be with us for evermore.

Matt.28.20
Rev.1.18
Heb.13.5,8

32. Salvation

i. What does the word mean?

It is a kind of 'portmanteau' word used in the Bible to describe our rescue from sin and our restoration to favour with God. It includes the many other technical words which are used, and which represent different aspects of our salvation — cleansing, forgiveness, redemption, justification.

Rom.1.16
1 John 1.7
Eph.1.7
Rom.5.1,9

ii. In what way do we need salvation?

a. The past. We need to be saved from the penalty of sin.

Eph.2.8-10
Titus 2.14
1 Pet.1.18.19

b. The present. Each day of our lives we need to be saved from its tyranny and power.

Rom.5.10; 6.14
1 Cor.1.18

c. The future. One day, when we go to be with Christ, we shall be saved from the actual presence of sin. We shall feel its influence no more.

Rom.13.11
1 Thess.5.9
1 Pet.1.5

iii. Why can't we save ourselves?

a. Because we cannot mend broken laws in the past with good resolutions for the future.

1 John 3.4
Gal.2.16
2 Tim.1.8,9

b. Because even our best deeds are so often riddled with pride and wrongly motivated that they fall far short of God's standard.

Deut.9.4-6
Isa.64.6

c. Because if we could rescue ourselves, we would become intolerably proud and priggish.

Eph.2.9

iv. How then can we be saved?

a. It stems from God's great love for his creatures, and the fact that he could not leave them to perish.

John 3.16
Rom.5.8
Titus 2.11

b. It was made possible by the perfect sacrifice of himself which Jesus made upon the cross.

Matt.20.28
Col.1.14
Heb.9.11-14, 24-28

c. It may be enjoyed and experienced by faith: claiming our individual share in what he has done, putting our trust in him, and receiving him as our personal Saviour.

Acts 16.30,31
Rom.1.16
Eph.2.8-10

33. Service

i. How can we serve Christ?

a. By the kind of life we live we can advertize him in the world, as his ambassadors.	Matt.5.16 2 Cor.5.20 1 Thess.1.5,6
b. By speaking to others, writing to them or lending them books, we can help them towards an understanding of the truth.	John 1.35-51 Acts 8.29-40 Acts 9.10-18
c. Our prayers can influence the course of events, and prepare the hearts of people to receive the gospel.	Matt.9.37,38 Luke 22.32 2 Cor.1.11 2 Thess.3.1
d. If we are in a position to do so, we can give money to help the spread of the gospel.	Heb.13.18 Ex.36.5-7 Luke 8.3
e. We may even be able to choose a career which will enable us to spend much of our time in Christian activities.	Luke 21.1-4 1 Tim.6.17-19 Acts 13.2
f. By doing our ordinary work to the glory of God.	Eph.6.5-7 Col.3.23

ii. Why should we serve Christ?

a. Because Christ has done so much for us, we should want to serve him in return.	2 Cor.5.14
b. Because others need Christ, and perhaps we are the only way in which they can hear about him.	Ezek.33.1-9 2 Cor.4.3,4
c. Because in serving him we shall find a life of satisfaction and purpose for ourselves.	John 4.34-38

34. Sex

i. What is wrong with sex?

Nothing! It is one of the greatest gifts which God has bestowed upon men and women, and which he wants us to use aright and to enjoy.

Gen.1.27,28
Gen.2.18
Eccles.9.9
Prov.5.18,19

ii. Then what can go wrong with sex?

Just as the abuse of God's other gifts can turn a person into a glutton, a gambler or a drunkard, so it is possible for us to misuse the gift of sex, and the Bible makes it perfectly plain that all sexual intimacy outside the marriage relationship is forbidden:

a. Adultery, when at least one of the people taking part in such intimacy is already married.

b. Fornication, when neither person is married.

Ex.20.14
Deut.22.22
Prov.6.29,32
Mark 7.21
1 Cor.6.18
1 Thess.4.3

c. Homosexuality, which is the word used to describe sexual relations when both people are of the same sex.

Lev.18.22
Rom.1.25-29
1 Cor.6.9

d. Bestiality, when a human being is involved in sexual relations with an animal.

Lev.18.23

35. Sin

i. What is sin?

There are many definitions of sin in the Bible, but three principal words are used.

a. Sin. The first is the word 'sin' itself. Originally it meant to fall short, or to miss the mark. Rom.3.22,23

b. Iniquity. Literally the word means 'uneven' or 'unjust', like the ragged and twisted line that results when we try to mark out a tennis court without a cord to guide us. Psa.51 Isa.53.6 1 John 5.17

c. Transgression or *trespass.* This means the breaking of God's law in thought, word and deed: crossing the boundary he has set for human behaviour. 1 John 3.4

ii. Does sin matter?

a. It spoils people's lives and the world in which we live, bringing sorrow and suffering in its wake. Isa.1.4-6 Mark 7.21-23 Rom.8.19-22

b. It binds people, and makes prisoners of them, so that they cannot break free from the habits they have formed. John 8.34 Rom.6.17

c. It separates man from God, because he is utterly holy, and must banish everything sinful from his presence for ever. Isa.59.1,2 Rom.6.23

iii. Can anything be done about it?

The chief reason why Jesus came into the world was to deal with the problem of sin, to remove its guilt and to break its power. Matt.1.21 Luke 4.18 1 Tim.1.15 1 John 4.10,14

36. Social Responsibility

i. Is the Christian under an obligation to help people socially?

It is true that much of what the Church used to do in the way of social relief is now done by the state, and is paid for out of rates and taxes. It is also true that the Christian will want to devote most of his energy and money to specifically spiritual work which can be supported by no one else. But no Christian should be able to see suffering, poverty or distress without wanting to do something to help.

Psa.41.1
Prov.31.20
Matt.25.31-46
1 John 3.17

ii. What can he do?

a. He can seize the opportunities which are sure to come, just as they came to the good Samaritan on his journey to Jericho. Luke 10.30-37 Heb.13.1-3

b. He can undertake some regular social work. James 1.27

c. He can devote part of the money he sets aside for God's work to relieve the material wants of people in need. 2 Cor.8 & 9 1 Tim.6.17,18

d. He can agitate at local and national levels for the reform of social evils. Amos 4.1-3

37. Suffering

i. What do we mean by suffering?

We must distinguish three different kinds of suffering to which we are prone.

a. That which is brought about by our own human folly, selfishness and sin for which we alone must accept responsibility. Isa.1.4-9 James 4.1-3

b. That which seems to have no human cause floods, volcanoes, and so on — and which Jesus himself said had no connexion with human sin. Luke 13.1-5

c. That which comes to Christians because of their faith in, and loyalty to, Christ. 1 Pet.4.12-16

ii. Why does God allow suffering?

There is, in this life, no completely satisfying answer that we can find in the Bible to this question, and the Christian takes refuge in the belief that one day God will explain everything to us. Meanwhile, he is sustained by the following thoughts. 1 Cor.13.12

a. That in the end, in the next life if not in this one, those who have suffered will find some form of compensation. Rom.8.28 Luke 16.25 Rev.7.14-17

b. That for those who have faith in God's goodness, suffering can be the means of drawing them closer to himself, and deepening their love and trust in him. James 1.2-4, 12 1 Pet.1.3-7

c. That the existence of suffering, sorrow and pain draws out from people courage, compassion and sympathy which might otherwise find no form of expression. Luke 10.30-35

38. Temptation

i. What is it?

Temptation is the urge which we all feel at times to do what we know to be wrong — what is forbidden in the Bible or against the dictates of our own conscience.	James 1.14,15

ii. Where does it come from?

a. Sometimes it comes from within, from what Paul called 'the flesh', meaning our human nature with its innate bias towards sin.	Rom.7.18-25 Gal.5.17
b. Sometimes it comes from without, as a direct attack upon us by Satan himself, 'the Devil'.	Gen.3 Matt.4.1-11
c. Sometimes it comes from around, from the influence of other people, from what the Bible refers to as 'the world'.	2 Tim.4.10 1 John 2.14-17

iii. Why does God allow it?

We must remember that God does not cause temptation, but he does allow it, because it is a way in which we learn to be more dependent upon him, better able to help others, and stronger in faith.	James 1.2,3, 12,13

iv. How can we overcome it?

a. We must be quite confident that victory is promised, and therefore possible.	1 Cor.10.13 1 Cor.15.57
b. We must be humble, vigilant and continually on our guard, never taking success for granted.	Matt.26.41 1 Cor.10.12 1 Pet.5.8,9
c. We must keep away from areas where we know temptation lies in wait for us.	1 Thess.4.22
d. We must soak ourselves in the Bible so that we can use it, as Jesus did, as a sword against temptation.	Psa.119.11 Matt.4.1-11 Eph.6.17
e. We must pray at all times, and especially in the moment of attack.	Eph.6.18 Matt.26.41 Matt,14.30
f. We must trust in Christ to give us the power we need when the fight is on.	1 John 4.4 1 John 5.4

39. The World

i. In what senses does the Bible use this word?

a. The created universe, brought into existence by the word of God, and sustained by his wisdom and power. Gen.1.1 Psa.24.1 Psa.65.6-13 Heb.1.3

b. The sum total of human beings who inhabit the earth. John 1.29; 3.16 Rom.1.8; 3.19

c. Society organised without reference to God. This is a very specialized use of the word, confined to the New Testament, and particularly to the writings of John. It is as nearly as possible the direct opposite of the Church, of which Christ is the Head and the centre. John 16.33; 17.9 1 John 2.15-17

ii. How are we to relate to the world in this last sense?

a. We must not isolate ourselves from it. Not only is this virtually impossible to do, but it would eliminate any influence for good we might have. It would extinguish the light, and remove the salt of the earth. Matt.5.13-16 John 17.15 1 Cor.5.9,10 Phil.2.15

b. On the other hand we must not identify ourselves with it, and allow ourselves to be moulded by its standards, values and customs. If we do, the salt will lost its distinctive flavour, and once again our influence will disappear. Rom.12.1,2 2 Tim.4.10 James 4.4 1 John 2.15-17

c. Somewhere between these two extremes is the path the Christian must find and tread — *in the world, but not of it.* To help us we have the example of Jesus himself who was known as 'a friend of sinners', and yet never mistaken for one, and recognized as 'separate from sinners'. Matt.11.19 Heb.7.26

40. Worship

i. What do we mean by worship?

The word really means 'worth-ship', and it includes anything we do or say which shows how much we value and respect God. In modern usage the word has become rather narrowed to mean the homage and respect we pay to God, either individually or congregationally, in prayer, praise and song.

Gen.24.26
1 Chron.29.20
Rev.4.11; 5.12

ii. Is all worship pleasing to God?

If it is to be really acceptable to him:

a. It must come from hearts that are cleansed from sin, and right with him.

1 Chron.16.29
Psa.66.18

b. It must be sincere — that is, the words of ourlips must be matched with the thoughts of our hearts.

Isa.29.13
John 4.24

c. It must be humble, reverent and offered with a sense of awe and wonder.

Heb.12.28
Rev.1.17